10½

LESSONS
FROM
EXPERIENCE

10 ½

LESSONS
FROM
EXPERIENCE

PERSPECTIVES
ON FUND
MANAGEMENT

PAUL
MARSHALL

**PROFILE
EDITIONS**

First published in Great Britain in 2020 by
Profile Editions, an imprint of
Profile Books Ltd
29 Cloth Fair
London EC1A 7JQ
www.profilebooks.com

Copyright © Paul Marshall 2020

1 3 5 7 9 10 8 6 4 2

The moral right of the author has been asserted.

All rights reserved. Without limiting the rights under copyright reserved above, no part of this publication may be reproduced, stored or introduced into a retrieval system, or transmitted, in any form or by any means (electronic, mechanical, photocopying, recording or otherwise), without the prior written permission of both the copyright owner and the publisher of this book.

All reasonable efforts have been made to obtain copyright permissions where required. Any omissions and errors of attribution are unintentional and will, if notified in writing to the publisher, be corrected in future printings.

A CIP catalogue record for this book is available from the British Library.

ISBN 978 1 78816 623 2

Typeset in Elena by MacGuru Ltd
Printed and bound in Britain by Clays Ltd, Elcograf S.p.A.

CONTENTS

Preface   vii

Introduction: The Great Disconnect	1
Lesson 1: Markets are inefficient	9
Lesson 2: Humans are irrational	21
Lesson 3: Investment skill is measurable and persistent	39
Lesson 4: In the short term the market is a voting machine, in the long term it is a weighing machine	47
Lesson 5: Seek change	53
Lesson 6: The best portfolio construction combines Concentration with Diversification	61
Lesson 7: Shorts are different from longs	69
Lesson 8: A machine beats a man, but a man plus a machine beats a machine	79

Lesson 9: Risk management – respect
   uncertainty   87
Lesson 10: Size matters   105
Lesson 10½: Most fund management
   careers end in failure   111

Glossary   117

PREFACE

Ian Wace and I founded Marshall Wace 21 years ago. We have lived and invested through several cycles and much turbulence, including LTCM, the internet bubble and crash, 9/11, the Great Moderation, the Great Financial Crisis, the Euro Crisis, 'Whatever it takes' and QE to Infinity. We have made mistakes along the way, but over time we have forged an investment model combining fundamental and systematic equity long/short strategies which is pretty much unique around the world. It is a model which achieves robustness through diversification and through the combined efforts of a deep bench of talented investors and analysts. And it has enabled Marshall Wace to become one of the world's more successful hedge fund businesses.

We have learned many lessons through the years, and my own evolving thoughts on investing have been pruned and rounded, developing into a set of perspectives which have in turn helped in shaping and measuring the development of others within Marshall Wace.

This small publication attempts to describe some of these perspectives. It is not intended to be comprehensive, nor is it intended to be formulaic. The nature of investing is that to be successful you need to constantly adapt. Markets and market participants are continuously evolving. To beat the markets, to generate alpha, you have to beat the other participants. And as they change, so you too need to evolve. That is why I call them 'lessons from experience'. We keep learning.

Marshall Wace was not built on these lessons. Neither Ian nor I would suggest they were the original building blocks of the investment business. Nonetheless, they have played their part, implicitly or explicitly, in the way we have thought about the challenges we have faced over time and in the way we have shaped the business, especially on the fundamental side.

Central to the success of any investment management business, and most certainly to Marshall Wace, are the processes and systems which support the investment management activity. Our business would not have succeeded without the investments we have made in optimisation, trading, technology and operating systems. Investment 'alpha' is always reported net of trading costs and stock lending costs. Relative to our competitors our low-cost structure is an integral factor in the strength of our alpha. It is the genius of my partner, Ian, that he always understood the vital role played by systems and infrastructure and had the vision and passion to invest in them.

Ultimately, any investment management firm is dependent on the commitment and confidence of its clients. We are their servants – and it is only thanks to their unfailing support for over twenty years that we have been able to invest, deliver and evolve.

INTRODUCTION: THE GREAT DISCONNECT

In theory there is no difference between theory and practice. In practice there is.
(Yogi Berra)

There can be no field of human knowledge where the disconnect between theory and practice is as pronounced as finance.

Financial theorists build models on the basis that markets are rational and efficient. Many practitioners have been able to build fortunes out of the fact that they are not.

Most of the theory which has accumulated to explain and predict markets is axiomatic and reductive. Yet it is supposed to be applied to a domain which is complex, constantly evolving, and unpredictable.

Axioms and reductive assumptions

provide shortcuts to understanding complex systems. If they work, of course, even for most of the time, they can deliver huge benefits (and profits). Axiomatic thinking can be effective and can stand the test of time in a domain like physics or pure maths, where the objects of the theory are inanimate or mechanical. But axiomatic thinking is inherently dangerous in the social sciences – basically in any domain which involves human agency in the systems you are trying to model or predict.

Axiomatic thinking is the ugly child of the Enlightenment. From its earliest days, the Enlightenment traced two paths, what you might call the Scottish path and the French path. The claims of science as advanced by David Hume were inherently modest:

> There is nothing in any object, consider'd in itself, which can afford us a reason for drawing a conclusion beyond it ... even after the observation of the frequent or constant conjunction of objects, we have no reason to draw any inference

concerning any object beyond those of which we have had experience.

(Hume, *A Treatise of Human Nature*, 1739–40)

Scottish thinkers (Hutcheson, Hume, Smith) were empiricists – they chose to advance with humility, tentatively, and on the basis of what worked.

In contrast, the tradition of French philosophy was, almost from its beginnings, rational, deductive and reductive. French thinkers – like Descartes, Rousseau, Walras – preferred to start with axioms and then seek out the evidence to prove them.

To be fair, this was not purely a French trait. One of the most formative thinkers in the development of Enlightenment economics was the Englishman, William Jevons, who perhaps more than any other was responsible for using the methods of maths and physics to try to turn economics into a science. It was Jevons who introduced the idea of quantifying the feelings of pleasure and pain and established the theory of marginal utility. Another Englishman, the philosopher John Stuart Mill, is credited with the step of reducing man to a purely economic entity (*homo economicus*) for the purposes of his political theory:

> Political economy does not treat the whole of man's nature as modified by the social state, nor of the whole conduct of man in society. It is concerned with him solely as a being who desires to possess wealth, and who is capable of judging the comparative efficacy of means for obtaining that.
> (Mill, *On the Definition of Political Economy*, 1836)

The axiomatic, or what some call Rationalist, tradition has continued to flourish in the post-Second World War period, led by the Chicago School, and it remains to this day remarkably disconnected from financial market practice. It is facing increasing challenge, though, not least from behavioural economics and from a new school called 'complexity economics'. In 1987 the Santa Fe Institute founded this new discipline, and

INTRODUCTION: THE GREAT DISCONNECT

in one of their inaugural sessions organised a ten-day meeting to discuss economics. On one side, they invited leading economists such as Kenneth Arrow and Larry Summers; on the other side, they invited physicists, biologists and computer scientists such as Nobel-winning Philip Anderson and John Holland. When the economists explained their assumptions, Phil Anderson said to them, 'You guys really believe that?' Sadly most of them still do.

This disconnect between academia and the real world exists in all social sciences – economics, politics, sociology, psychology. In all of these fields, the reductive thinking which has held sway for 200 years is now starting to be unpicked, and we are entering a period which can best be described – in a good way – as post-Enlightenment.

The timing of this post-Enlightenment is not a coincidence. Science is impatient. It measures what it can with the tools in its possession. Its main tool is mathematics. The kind of mathematics which was fundamental to the Industrial Revolution was basically linear in nature; predictable inputs led to proportionate outputs and axiomatic reasoning could be extended into the physical world. The success of calculus, linear and dynamic programming, and the equations of physics and engineering, however, meant that they were extended into many domains which they could not fully explain.

The big change is that now computational power is becoming available to deal with much greater complexity – with problems which are non-linear and multi-agent. We no longer have to rely on so many axioms.

The inadequacy of Enlightenment thinking is especially true in relation to markets, because markets are an exemplar of what cannot be contained within axiomatic thought. They are highly complex non-linear systems created by a myriad of half-informed or uninformed decisions made by fallible (human) agents with multiple cognitive biases.

All the simplifying axioms of finance contain a large element of truth and applicability, otherwise their authors would not have alighted upon them and they would not have gained traction with practitioners. But all have exceptions (or flaws) and it is generally the exceptions which are interesting, rather than the rules.

In the end, the axioms are no better than falsifying assumptions. Understanding why they are falsifying is the beginning of financial wisdom.

In setting out these ten lessons, I have felt it necessary to start by taking on the axiomatic pillars of academic theory. The first two lessons may seem like motherhood and apple pie to market practitioners, but they need to be stated because they are so at odds with the theory of change which prevails in universities and business schools. Graduate recruits from academia face a sharp learning curve when they confront the realities of the market. If they do not adapt quickly, the results can be catastrophic (just ask Robert Merton and Myron Scholes).

The first two lessons need stating because you have to get your foundations right. In the spirit of John Locke, it is necessary to clear the ground of stones and rubble before anything useful can be either built or planted there. Subsequent lessons after these two are more rooted in our own practice, learned and honed over the years from successes and failures.

LESSON 1
MARKETS ARE INEFFICIENT

The falsifying assumptions behind efficient market theory began with the Frenchman Léon Walras.

Léon Walras started his career as a physicist, and attempted to extend the axiomatic method into economics. In his *Elements d'Economie Politique Pure* of 1877, he originated the general equilibrium theory, which stated that the total excess demand in an economy had to equal the total excess supply, and that in equilibrium both quantities would equal zero. It is a theory which has unlocked many further innovations in economics but, as anyone who has worked in any market at all knows, it works much better in theory than in practice. Supply and demand are virtually never in complete equilibrium. Disequilibria are resolved through price movements. Sometimes, in the case of excess supply, price movements are not enough to create equilibrium. A stock of surplus inventory is just left unsold. The opportunities to make money in business and in markets lie precisely in the points of disequilibrium.

It was a small step from Walras to Louis Bachelier, a French mathematician, who imported the principles of general equilibrium theory into financial markets. Bachelier developed the theory of the random walk, which assumes that from any starting point prices go up or down with equal probability in the same way that a coin-toss is equally likely to produce heads or tails. Bachelier's founding assumption allowed him to apply the traditional laws of probability to price movements, crucially the law of 'normal distribution'.

Bachelier's work was developed further by Eugene Fama in the 1960s into the efficient-market hypothesis (EMH), which holds that in an 'ideal' market all relevant information is priced into a security – and that yesterday's price does not influence today's or tomorrow's.

Fama produced no quantitative measure of market efficiency and not much empirical evidence. Testing his hypothesis is therefore difficult.

Fama and his successors tended to argue from the established fact that most American mutual funds underperform the S&P500, to the conclusion that no other investor could outperform any market. Fama distinguished between 'weak' (past prices do not influence the future), 'semi-strong' (public information about fundamentals cannot be used to predict prices) and 'strong' (no prediction is possible, even with inside information) forms of his theory, but usually tested the weaker ones and acted as if he had proved the stronger ones.

Efficient-market theory is so far removed from working reality that it has become the butt of many jokes, of which my favourite is probably the following:

Two economists are walking down

the street. One spots a $100 bill on the ground. 'Hey,' he says to his friend, 'there's a hundred bucks lying on the ground!' 'Don't be silly,' the other replies, 'if there were a hundred dollars on the ground, someone would have picked it up already!'

Fama's 'ideal world' does not exist. Information is only ever partially available and despite the best efforts of regulators to create a level playing field, that information is available in very varying degrees to different participants. At the simplest level, professional investors always have better and easier access to more information than retail investors. For this reason, professional investors seek out markets where there is a high retail component because they know there will be richer alpha (China vs. US).

Prices can also move a very long way from fair value, simply due to mismatches of supply and demand. This is best illustrated by what is called the 'scarcity paradox', first set out by Adam Smith.

LESSON 1

What are the rules which men naturally observe in exchanging them [goods] for money or for one another, I shall now proceed to examine. These rules determine what may be called the relative or exchangeable value of goods. The word VALUE, it is to be observed, has two different meanings, and sometimes expresses the utility of some particular object, and sometimes the power of purchasing other goods which the possession of that object conveys. The one may be called 'value in use;' the other, 'value in exchange.' The things which have the greatest value in use have frequently little or no value in exchange; on the contrary, those which have the greatest value in exchange have frequently little or no value in use. Nothing is more useful than water: but it will purchase scarcely anything; scarcely anything can be had in exchange for it. A diamond, on the contrary, has scarcely any use-value; but a very great quantity of other goods may frequently be had in exchange for it.
(Smith, *The Wealth of Nations*, 1776)

Water and diamonds may attract vastly different prices depending on the circumstances of the buyer/seller. A starving man in the desert may pay almost any price (certainly all of his diamonds) for a glass of water. His price elasticity is almost infinite. In normal circumstances, on the other hand, where water is in abundant supply, he would expect to pay almost nothing, and certainly not sacrifice any diamonds. There are many illustrations of the scarcity paradox – for example, in general conditions, LIBOR funding is a plentiful and cheap commodity, but in 2008 after the collapse of Lehman Brothers, it became scarce and so precious that people were prepared to destroy their reputations and careers in order to secure access to it.

Price formation happens with varying degrees of inefficiency, and price formation is typically volatile and non-linear.

In recent years, various thinkers have emerged who have rejected efficient-market theory and explored models which come closer to approximating market reality.

These voices typically have emerged from outside the echo chambers of academia – they are mainly practitioners or lone wolves – and so have not been given a particularly warm welcome in 'Enlightenment' circles. Two stand out.

Benoit Mandelbrot
Mandelbrot was another Frenchman, but a Polish Jew by birth. He has shown that in many financial markets, price movements do not have the same well-behaved probability distributions that you find in physics. The 'tails' of the distributions are 'fat' because extreme price moves happen much more often than they would if the market were described by the conventional bell curve. Anyone who works in markets will know from experience that Mandelbrot is right. If the normal distribution was a good way to think about market risk, the probability of the 29.2 per cent fall in the Dow Jones index on 19 October 1987 would have been less than 1 in 10^{50}; as close to zero as one can imagine. During the August 2007 quant crash, we

had to listen to efforts by Goldman Sachs finance director David Viniar to justify his flagship quant funds' underperformance by reference to '26 standard deviation events'. Not me, guv, it is the markets that are not behaving!

Mandelbrot also had a good explanation for these fat tails. While Fama (and other Walrasians, going back to the inventor of the random walk theory, Louis Bachelier) had assumed that prices moved independently of each other, Mandelbrot argued that prices had a memory, of sorts. Today does, in fact, influence tomorrow. And different price series exhibit different degrees of memory. Mandelbrot chose not to try to explain why today's price may influence tomorrow's. But the obvious explanation, obvious at least to anyone who works in markets, is that market participants are human beings, and humans, driven by fear and greed, are swayed by price movements.

George Soros
You could say that George Soros went one

step further than Mandelbrot with his theory of reflexivity. He argued that not only do prices influence other prices but they actually influence fundamentals in a feedback loop. Markets not only anticipate economic developments but actually drive them and are in turn driven by them, because 'human beings are not merely scientific observers but also active participants in the system'. With his theory of reflexivity, Soros was demonstrating the limits to understanding and predictability in a self-referential system, a system where an observer is part of what he is observing.

The theory of reflexivity is best illustrated by the classic emerging market phenomenon of contagion (for example, Turkey in 2018). An emerging market country with a high budget deficit and high levels of foreign currency (dollar) debt experiences a speculative attack on its currency. The fall in the currency causes the dollar debt to rise further as a share of domestic GDP, aggravating the situation. The depreciation in the currency in turn leads to higher inflation, which leads to further speculation against the currency and a further rise in the share of dollar debt to GDP. The combination of a falling currency and rising inflation puts pressure on the central bank to raise interest rates and this in turn puts pressure on real assets. A vicious circle is induced.

Inefficiencies and anomalies
Market inefficiencies are visible every day to practitioners. But the anomalies do not automatically close. The challenge is having the conviction and the staying power and the process to exploit them. There can be occasions when valuation anomalies persist for months or years or even decades. The most important corrective in equity markets is a properly functioning market for corporate control. Ultimately, if a company becomes too cheap and the value margin becomes too appetising, a corporate buyer will step in to take advantage – providing, of course, that the governance mechanisms allow it.

Probably, the best case that can be made by supporters of the efficient-market hypothesis is that markets are growing more efficient over time. Professionalisation is the main reason. The retail share of stock market trading falls steadily as markets gain in maturity. The retail share in the US fell from 50 per cent in 1970 to 15 per cent today. China's retail share today is, by contrast, still 85 per cent.

Professional investors access far more information than retail investors, from company accounts, through to liquidity flow data, technicals, and now alternative data. They process it better and faster and analyse it better and faster (with increasing use of machines in both cases). In the world of quantitative strategies, the shelf life of new 'alpha opportunities' is shortening as more and better investors (with the help of machines) move to exploit them faster.

The biggest symptom of the failure of active fund management is the growth in index funds. These have quintupled between 2009 and 2019 and at the time of writing (2020) stand at over $10 trillion. Some would argue that the growth of index funds makes markets more inefficient, as index investing is little more than a version of lagged momentum (index trackers add to shares which have done well and sell shares which have done badly). The alternative argument is that the growth of indexation is coming at the expense of weaker active managers. The best analogy is a poker game where the poorer players lose their money and drop out first. Arguably, that makes the game harder for the more skilled players that remain, not easier. It certainly results in less liquidity and index funds only trade by (quarterly) appointment.

In any event, even if the battlefield is more intense, the inefficiencies remain. Perhaps the best evidence of market inefficiency is the persistence of skill (see Lesson 3), something which Eugene Fama would never be willing to acknowledge.

LESSON 2
HUMANS ARE IRRATIONAL

If there is one reason to be grateful to social media, it is that it has demonstrated once and for all that people are not rational. Loyalty to tribe is much more powerful than loyalty to truth. As Pascal wrote in his *Pensées* of 1670, 'Le cœur a ses raisons que la raison ne connaît point'.

Yet the assumption of human rationality is a foundation stone of Enlightenment economics and of the efficient-market hypothesis in particular. It originated with Frenchman René Descartes, but its lineage can be traced through economists and financial academics from Utilitarians, like Mill, to Robert Lucas, who developed the theory of rational expectations. Lucas provided an ingenious twist to the EMH and enabled Rationalists to retain their grip on financial theory by assuming that even if individuals might be irrational (which they manifestly are) in isolation, on average the population as a whole arrives at rational outcomes and that whenever new relevant information appears, the agents update their expectations appropriately. So now rational expectations theory does not require that the individual agents be rational. But it makes the overriding claim that, in aggregate, markets behave as if individual agents were rational – prices follow a random walk and market prices cannot be reliably exploited to make an abnormal profit. Shazam!

In its simplifying assumption of overall averaged-out rational behaviour, rational expectations theory conveniently steps over the fact that individual market participants on their own can often be *extremely* irrational. This makes for pretty weak science.

Fortunately, one or two more recent thinkers have developed theories of human behaviour which are anchored in observation and have more direct application to markets. Some were market practitioners, others not:

Fallibility

George Soros's theory of reflexivity was based on a prior assumption. This was the principle of fallibility.

> In situations that have thinking participants, the participants' views of the world never perfectly correspond to the actual state of affairs. People can gain knowledge of individual facts, but when it comes to formulating theories or forming an overall view, their perspective is bound to be either biased or inconsistent or both. That is the principle of fallibility.
>
> (Soros, 'Fallibility, Reflexivity and the Human Uncertainty Principle', *Journal of Economic Methodology*, 2013)

Fragility

Hyman Minsky was an American academic, not from the Chicago School. His focus was on the causes of financial crises and this led him to explore how fragility accumulated in human systems. His central insight was that long periods of financial stability could ultimately lead to instability because they promoted complacency and excessive leverage and risk-taking. Paul McCulley of PIMCO first coined the phrase 'Minsky moment' in relation to the Russian financial crisis of 1998. But an even better example of the phenomenon was the financial crisis of 2007–8, as this collapse stemmed in many ways from the 'Great Moderation', the period of extended financial buoyancy created by the monetary accommodation of Alan Greenspan and leading to the accumulation of too much leverage and speculation throughout the financial system.

The same principle can work the other way. An extreme financial crisis may engender a prolonged period of stability because of the resultant risk aversion among not only market participants but also institutional authorities.

Arguably, the exceptional period of

financial stability following the Great Financial Crisis was a Minsky moment in reverse, as market participants were slow to redeploy risk, but more importantly, authorities and central banks did everything in their power to assure stability for asset prices. They should of course have known better. Financial authorities can never guarantee the stability of financial markets and all that the excessive period of QE has done is sow the seeds of the next Minsky moment when financial support is withdrawn.

In general, the Minsky cycle describes a repetitive chain of financial crises punctuated by intervening stability, all driven by a recognisable and predictable pattern of human behaviour. In that sense, the insights are not startling but they have the advantage of being grounded in observable human behaviour.

A rather more modest version of the Minsky cycle is the CRIC cycle, a term coined by Morgan Stanley to describe the endlessly repetitive crises within the Eurozone, starting in 2011:

Crisis-Response-Improvement-Complacency. Complacency should never have been allowed, given the inherent flaws of a currency union of divergent economies without either fiscal union or banking union. But complacency was often in the ascendant, not only among the politicians but even among investors, who were often either just exhausted or just bored by the risks. Complacency eventually paved the way for a Crisis, which then drew a Response, primarily from the ECB (LTROs, TLTROs, OMTs, 'Whatever it takes'...). The markets took comfort from the response, leading to a period of Improvement followed in due course by renewed Complacency until the underlying flaws reared their head again in a financial Crisis. The CRIC cycle anchors market movements in observable patterns of human behaviour, similar to the Minsky cycle.

Stupidity
There is no such thing as a Stupidity Principle but there should be. Stupidity is a very basic symptom of the human condition.

LESSON 2

People can be equipped with all necessary information but still make the wrong decision. We all make decisions that we come to view as stupid with hindsight.

Stupidity is better understood (or acknowledged) by novelists than by Enlightenment philosophers. Flaubert saw stupidity as an enduring feature of human existence:

> It accompanies poor Emma throughout her days, to her bed of love and to her deathbed. Stupidity does not give way to science, technology, modernity, progress: on the contrary, it progresses right along with progress.
>
> (Flaubert, *Madame Bovary*, 1857)

It was equally understood by Dostoevsky and Hannah Arendt. But it was harder for Bachelier, Walras or Fama. You can't model stupidity. It does not conform to any predictable rules.

Behavioural biases

The most important challenge to the

assumption of human rationality has come from Danny Kahneman. It should perhaps be no surprise that the challenge should have come from outside the traditional academic economics discipline, nor that the discipline concerned should be behavioural psychology. The work of Danny Kahneman and of Amos Tversky has been revolutionary for finance. And because it is rooted in empirical research it is likely to endure.

Marshall Wace has used Kahneman's lexicon of cognitive biases both to evaluate our own fund managers and to evaluate and coach our TOPS* contributors. A few examples give a flavour of how it has worked for us:

Optimism bias is one of the most commonly occurring biases. It is technically

---

* TOPS ('Trade-Optimised Portfolio System') is the name given to Marshall Wace's 'alpha capture' strategy, in which we ask outside contributors from the brokerage community to input their best ideas into an online portal which allows us to track their performance and to identify those contributors who have reliable information to offer.

defined as 'a cognitive bias which causes a person to believe that they are at a lesser risk of experiencing a negative event compared to others'. I suffer from it, not only in relation to my own personal circumstances but also to my investments. I am too easily romanced by new stories and new opportunities and will too often want to go with the momentum of an idea until the momentum breaks.

The **gambler's fallacy** (also known as the Monte Carlo fallacy or the fallacy of the maturity of chances) is the belief that, if something happens more frequently than normal during a given period, it will happen less frequently in the future (or vice versa). It is naturally attributable to roulette but is a clear parallel to the view that stocks will always revert to their mean.

Applying gambler's fallacy to financial markets might be termed **mean reversion bias**. This does not earn a mention under that name in Kahneman's official lexicon but it should do, especially as it is the main cognitive bias of my co-founder, Ian Wace.

Ian's primary interest in financial markets is in exploiting the moments of exuberance or distress in the markets on the basis that they create pricing anomalies which will quickly be erased. His basic assumption no doubt reflects his first fifteen years' experience as a broker/trader when he was used to taking the other side to the excessive optimism/pessimism of his counterparties.

Optimism bias and the gambler's fallacy/mean reversion bias map in their respective ways on to the style factors which have become the staple of most risk models and risk premium businesses, namely momentum and value. My portfolios will almost always have a bias towards medium-term momentum unless I deliberately hedge it out. Ian's book more often than not had a bias to value. Taken together our style biases were a good hedge to each other. They could also from time to time be a source of real tension!

Overconfidence results in 'the false assumption that an individual is superior to others, due to their own false sense of skill,

LESSON 2

talent, or self-belief'. It is prolific in finance and capital markets. The Greeks called it *hubris*. Because almost everyone is susceptible to it, it needs to be managed out of the system. When someone is doing well their portfolio should be subject to extra scrutiny and their ego deflated. When they are doing poorly they need to feel supported and have their ego boosted. Alex Ferguson employed this approach to man-management at Manchester United. David Beckham was a particular victim, most famously after he scored England's last-minute equaliser against Greece in 2001 to assure qualification for the World Cup Finals. Here is the *Guardian* newspaper:

> Such have been the superhuman qualities attributed to David Beckham since Saturday that it was tempting to wonder whether he joined his Manchester United colleagues on their flight to Athens yesterday or flew on his own alongside their plane, dressed in a red cape and blue tights.

Beckham-mania has undeniably reached new heights, but with every high there inevitably comes a low and one was duly provided here last night. That it came from Sir Alex Ferguson was wholly unexpected but, sure enough, in an extraordinary statement of intent the United manager revealed that he planned to drop England's captain from tonight's Group G encounter with Olympiakos because, among other things, Beckham might need bringing 'back down to earth'.

(Daniel Taylor, *Guardian*, 2001)

Anchoring bias occurs when someone allows an initial piece of information to sway subsequent judgements. This also applies to initial experiences – whether professional or emotional. One of our longest-serving (and highly successful) managers developed his investment approach in the years immediately preceding the financial crisis. He earned his spurs in 2008. One of his core portfolio behaviours was to always run a stable net market exposure of circa 30 per cent and to concentrate that exposure in the healthcare and consumer staple sectors. These 'defensive' sectors had hugely outperformed during the financial crisis and indeed had outperformed during other market downturns before that. This gave him confidence to run a net long exposure in these sectors even in a bear market. But this was not an optimal portfolio structure. No-one has decreed that net exposure should be stable at 30 per cent. Indeed, in a business which requires capital protection above all things and flexibility in market views, this static net market exposure (or 'lazy beta') was always a potential risk. Net exposure is one of the most valuable tools in a hedge fund manager's toolbox and should be used accordingly. There is nothing assured about the outperformance of defensive sectors, and in the 2010s, with increased disruption from the Internet, the consumer staple sector lost its previous properties. Yet it proved very difficult to shake the manager from his anchoring bias to 30 per cent net market exposure.

Another manager had learned his trade in a firm where he was only required to run 120 per cent gross gearing (that is, the sum of total longs plus total shorts, expressed as a proportion of the money under management). He became anchored to this behaviour despite the clear evidence – for years – that his returns would benefit from higher and more flexible gross gearing and that he could afford to run this larger hedged portfolio without incurring significant volatility.

Everyone suffers from **confirmation bias**, 'the tendency to interpret new evidence as confirmation of one's existing beliefs or theories'. It is a plague of social media and increasingly of the news media and politics, as people organise themselves into separate echo chambers. But it can also be a plague of a fund management business and it has to be countered by encouraging constant challenge. Managers and analysts need to specifically seek out contrary opinions and hold up their own theses to scrutiny. They need to know what their own biases are. They need to be challenged from within and without. By capturing almost every valid opinion on a stock in real time through our TOPS system, we at least give ourselves a chance of diminishing confirmation bias. You never get rid of it completely.

Disposition bias describes the tendency of investors to sell assets which have increased in value, while keeping assets which have dropped in value. This tendency is a frequent characteristic of TOPS contributors, and it requires us to demonstrate to them in very tangible ways (i.e. by showing them their portfolio results) that while they may have a very good success ratio (percentage of winning trades), they are not making commensurate returns because of their tendency to cut their winners and hold on to their losers.

In the real example shown in Figure 1 overleaf, you see the profile of a TOPS contributor with a very high success ratio (64.18 per cent) who nonetheless managed to deliver negative returns overall due to an acute disposition bias (selling his winners and holding on to his losers).

FIGURE 1 **Being right most of the time, but still losing money**

TOPS – Alpha Return Distribution (contributor example)

Success ratio: 64.18%   Average winner: 2.43%   Average loser: –4.54%

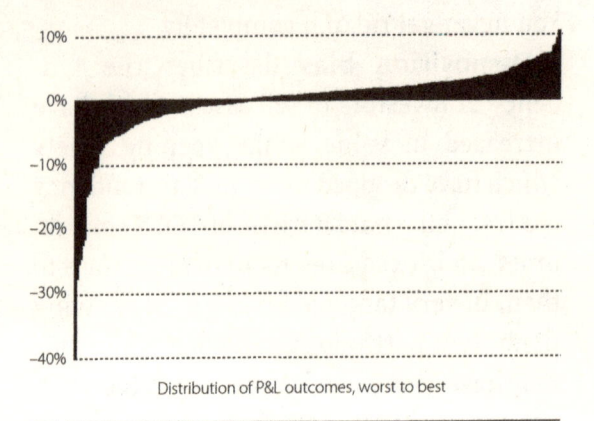

Distribution of P&L outcomes, worst to best

The **sunk cost fallacy** is sometimes known as the 'Concorde fallacy', in reference to the stubbornness of the British and French governments in continuing to fund the joint development of Concorde even after it became apparent that it was a commercial disaster. Decision makers were too heavily influenced by the fact they had already 'sunk costs' in the project, even though these costs should make no difference to ongoing investment decisions. Politicians are highly vulnerable to the sunk cost fallacy. It can be applied to a multitude of errors by the British government.

But there is a more subtle form of sunk cost fallacy, relating to the irrational weight given to the time an investor has spent analysing an opportunity. This must be even more of a temptation in private equity, where investors can spend weeks or months evaluating an opportunity. It is certainly true in public equity management. The main capacity constraint on an equity analyst is always his or her time. In any given day analysts have to decide which company to focus their time on, and before making the investment the analyst or fund manager will have spent many hours on the case. Given the amount of time consumed, it becomes increasingly difficult for the manager then to pass on the investment. But the time spent should be irrelevant. Analytical time should be viewed as a separate resource, with the expectation that only a certain percentage of opportunities will pass from due diligence to actual investment. Unfortunately, that is not normally how it happens.

The great achievement of Kahneman and Tversky was to demonstrate, through very substantial empirical research, that these behavioural biases were systematic and therefore applicable in practice. They are highly relevant and valuable to the art and science of fund management, and are deeply embedded in our practices, both as the discretionary and systematic side of the business.

These behavioural biases have received a muted reception from traditional academics. No doubt that is because Enlightenment economics is subject to its own very entrenched sunk cost fallacy. You don't want to blow up 200 years of ivory tower modelling by embracing too much reality.

LESSON 3
INVESTMENT SKILL IS MEASURABLE AND PERSISTENT

The way skill is measured in the fund management industry has evolved significantly over time. Thirty years ago it was largely a matter of just beating the index, without much attempt to look under the bonnet to understand how this was done. Most managers got away without much scrutiny, with performance records and reputations which could be based on a very small number of decisions or on one or two very dominant style bets. No doubt a few lounge lizards earned undeserved reputations.

Indeed, it would be interesting to dig below the surface of the performance records of some of the most revered investors of all time. How much was Peter Lynch's record based on a huge bias to small and mid-cap shares at a time (1980s) when these shares heavily outperformed the main market? How much is Warren Buffett's record based on a combination of leverage (his use of the insurance float allowed him to leverage his exposures close to two times) and market beta? His Sharpe Ratio in recent years is certainly very average.

Industry convention has now settled on two standard skill measures based on adjustments for risk – the Information Ratio (outperformance of benchmark)/(volatility of outperformance of benchmark) for long only managers and the Sharpe Ratio (absolute return in excess of the risk-free rate/volatility of absolute returns) for hedge fund managers. To have any confidence at all in the signalling power of these ratios you need at least three years and preferably five years of underlying daily data. And that period needs to have encompassed a variety of market regimes and ideally to include a bear market and not just a cruising bull market.

You can make a good career in fund management if your Information Ratio or Sharpe Ratio is consistently above 1× over time. Most Marshall Wace funds deliver Sharpe Ratios consistently above 1.5×.

But even these ratios are really only scratching the surface. It is now possible to dig much deeper into investment performance to separate the signal from the noise, the skill from the luck. Although a Sharpe Ratio above 1× over five years suggests a strong likelihood that you have found a good manager, you still don't know how much was due to a few outsized winning trades, how much was style bias, how much was regime dependent.

Luck is a key factor in fund management, just as it is in competitive sport. Michael Lewis has written a bestselling book (*Moneyball*) about how the Oakland A's evaluated their baseball players and how they separated skill from luck. Luck intervenes every day in market price formation, in terms of politics, unexpected corporate decisions, acts of God etc. But fortunately, we have a huge amount of data which we can use to separate the signal from the noise and thereby isolate skill.

We have found that the most important ratio for digging below the surface is the success ratio (the percentage of winning trades – the Americans call it the 'batting average'). We have for twenty years analysed each portfolio for its success ratio, both in relation to absolute returns and alpha. An alpha success ratio of 52–53 per cent is already very good if it is consistent through time. A truly great manager will have a success ratio of 55 per cent (in other words you can be wrong 45 per cent of the time and still be a truly great manager). Not only can we look at the overall success ratio, we can look at it by country, by sector, by longs, by shorts, in up markets and down markets, to build a deep profile over time of a manager's strengths and weaknesses and to establish his/her consistency.

It is possible to be a consistently good

manager with a success ratio below 50 per cent if you have a consistent skew towards winning stocks in your position sizing. Some managers are naturally good at concentrating their capital in their best ideas while their longer tail of diversifiers (which may be there more for risk management purposes) contains a high share of losers. These may reduce risk by more than they dilute returns. But you need to understand their role in the portfolio well before you give a manager a pass on a success ratio below 50 per cent.

You can go deeper still. It has for many years been possible to evaluate manager style biases (momentum, value, growth quality, size, volatility, etc.) and establish how much of the performance can be attributable to style and how much to pure 'idiosyncratic' skill. Some 'purist' fund management firms only credit skill to a manager if it is purely idiosyncratic (that is, with all style biases removed). We are not as hair-shirt as that but we do insist that at least 60 per cent of the risk for any given portfolio should be attributable to stock selection rather than exposure to country and style factors and we bear in mind the split between idiosyncratic skill and style-based performance when we evaluate a manager.

With this level of granularity and a vast pool of intra-day data on multiple managers and TOPS contributors stretching back over twenty years, we are able to identify persistent skill with a high degree of confidence.

The bad news for managers is that the frontiers for what can be defined as 'pure idiosyncratic skill' are being pushed further and further out. One definition of 'idiosyncratic' is simply 'that which cannot be explained'. You can now explain a lot of returns by reference to country and sector exposures, and style factors. Sector selection is a skill and therefore should arguably be regarded as idiosyncratic but it is now industry practice to treat it as a factor which can be explained away outside idiosyncratic stock picking. Some firms bar their managers from taking sector risk for these reasons. This is foolish. Industry selection is a demonstrable skill and cannot easily be replicated by machines (yet).

Other explicable or replicable factors are finding their ways into risk models, further reducing what can be deemed as idiosyncratic. Some managers now treat exposure to crowded shorts as a common risk and therefore to be excluded from the idiosyncratic component. This is 'hair shirt' performance attribution. Evaluating crowded short (and crowded long) exposure should definitely be a factor in risk management but should not be removed from the definition of idiosyncratic risk and return. After all, knowing when a short is genuinely crowded is part of the skill of long/short equity management. And this is a general point. Although risk management and performance attribution both use similar tools to break down overall portfolio risk into its components, the two purposes need to be kept logically and operationally distinct.

There is no particular set of attributes which can guarantee a great fund manager. Of course they have to be very smart, focused and driven. But great managers can be optimists, pessimists, mean reverters, growth guys, value guys, short-term traders and long-term holders.

Perhaps above all they have to be resilient. Despite the evidence of the persistence of skill there is probably not a single successful manager who has not had at least one bad year (Stanley Druckenmiller is the one exception I can think of). In that bad year, or that bad period, you come under huge pressure. Your mistakes are very public. You question yourself. Others question your judgement. You need to be resilient.

Indeed, the main threats to persistent performance are all character related and lie strictly speaking outside the domain of fund management. We have found, for example, that the reddest flags for underperformance in TOPS are problems in people's personal lives – the three Ds of death, divorce and disease.

LESSON 4
IN THE SHORT TERM THE MARKET IS A VOTING MACHINE, IN THE LONG TERM IT IS A WEIGHING MACHINE

Ben Graham is widely known as the father of 'value investing' and he is the originator of many important investment concepts, including 'margin of safety', concentrated diversification and activist investing. He also honourably acknowledged the constraints that size imposed on his style of value investing, something which his disciple Warren Buffett has never done.

However, what Graham should perhaps be respected for above all else is the emphasis he put on investor psychology. Despite being a master of security analysis (as per his book by that name*), he always left a lot of room for investor behaviour, as per his famous phrase 'in the short run the market is a voting machine, in the long term it is a weighing machine'.

Graham was in general fairly dismissive of short-term movements. The short-term market was a popularity contest to be exploited by traders. If anything, the short-term fluctuations just allowed him the opportunity to use his weighing machine to take advantage of the true value in companies. But at least he did leave space for, and acknowledge the importance of, short-term fluctuations.

Someone who paid a lot more respect to short-term market movements, though, was John Maynard Keynes.

Keynes was an economist who actually managed money – a rare thing. And he has an audited track record. He became bursar

---

*Security Analysis, co-authored with David Dodd.

LESSON 4

FIGURE 2 **Chest Fund Performance 1927 to 1946**

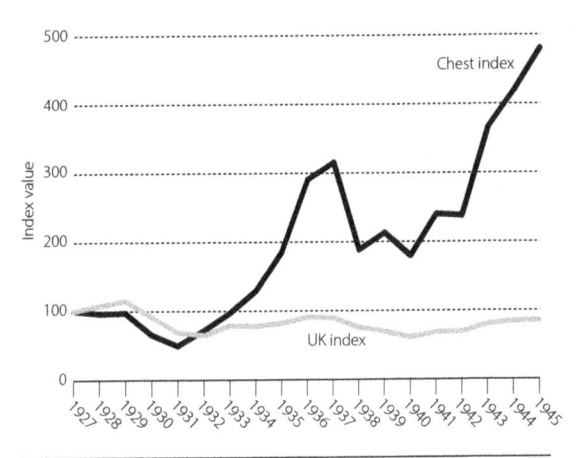

of King's College Cambridge in 1924 and from 1927 to 1946 was responsible for the College's Chest Fund. Over this period, the fund compounded at an annual return of 9.1 per cent while the UK stock market fell at an annualised rate of slightly less than 1 per cent (see Figure 2).

This was a remarkable performance, especially as Keynes could not use derivatives or hedges in the way modern managers can do. His weapons of choice were currencies and equities. Keynes showed almost unique foresight in understanding the economic consequences of Versailles and of the UK coming off gold in 1924. But it was not all plain sailing and he certainly had his setbacks (or as we call them today, drawdowns). Between 1928 and 1932 the Chest Fund fell substantially, and underperformed the UK equity market by a wide margin. But Keynes more than made up for it in the 1930s.

The reason Keynes is interesting as an investment seer is because he understood the interplay between fundamentals and the subjective mind. All of his famous sayings about the stock market relate to the nature of subjective thinking:

'Successful investing is anticipating the anticipations of others.'

'If farming were to be organised like the stock market, a farmer would sell his farm in the morning when it was raining, only to buy it back in the afternoon when the sun came out.'

Keynes's most famous investment

analogy likened investing to choosing the winner of a beauty contest. In the *General Theory* he imagined a newspaper competition where people were asked to choose the six most attractive faces from a collection of 100 faces. The person who identified the six most popular faces would win a prize. The task was not to identify the most attractive faces but to identify the faces which others would find the most attractive:

> It is not a case of choosing those [faces] that, to the best of one's judgment, are really the prettiest, nor even those that average opinion genuinely thinks the prettiest. We have reached the third degree where we devote our intelligences to anticipating what average opinion expects the average opinion to be. And there are some, I believe, who practice the fourth, fifth and higher degrees.
>
> (Keynes, *The General Theory of Employment, Interest and Money*, 1936)

For Marshall Wace the voting machine/

weighing machine duality goes to the heart of our business model. Indeed, you could say we have almost constructed the pillars of our business upon it. Our alpha capture (TOPS) and systematic (quant) trading businesses, which turn over between 8 and 15 times per year, are essentially in the voting machine game, exploiting and winning the popularity contests. Our fundamental managers (who have much longer holding periods) are in the weighing machine business, identifying and exploiting fundamental mis-valuations of companies. The two approaches exploit market inefficiencies over different time horizons. Both are profitable. Of course, our fundamental managers take account of sentiment and of investor flows, and of course, our alpha capture and systematic strategies take account of fundamentals. But Ben Graham's demarcation works as a description of our investment approach.

LESSON 5
SEEK CHANGE

If you assume that markets are on a path towards greater efficiency (the most that should ever be conceded to the Chicago School), it becomes critical to know where the greatest opportunities are to exploit inefficiencies. The greatest opportunities always occur around change. The valuation of a company will not change unless something changes intrinsically about the company (financially, operationally or strategically) or something changes about its economic/financial context (interest rates, growth, volatility, inflation) to create or destroy value.

Change is embodied in catalysts. These are the events, like takeovers, strategy announcements or new product launches, which announce to the market that something has happened and views need to be revised. That is why so many investors use a model based around 'valuation with a catalyst'.

The best exponents of this approach are event-driven managers who force concrete 'change', mostly in management or corporate structure, and make this the core driver of their investment approach. Some managers in this space such as Elliott or TCI have combined great investment returns with real improvements to the governance and management of the underlying companies. In an age where corporate governance has been so diluted by the agency problem, these managers should be greatly applauded. Other managers in the same space use the 'event-driven' approach more as a marketing gambit. They buy a stake in the company, write a letter to management proposing fairly cosmetic changes and hope that the excitement gives them enough margin to sell at a profit. They are not doing much more than advertising their investment thesis.

LESSON 5

Catalysts can matter simply because they create a story. Humans like stories. We are storytelling creatures. Since the earliest days when we sat around fires and told tales to give meaning to life and to pass that meaning down to our descendants, humankind has lived through stories. It is no different with markets. Investors respond to stories. Catalysts make the stories concrete. That is the other reason why 'value with a catalyst' is so effective as an investment approach. Provided that the stock has a claim to undervaluation and there is a path to how the value can be crystallised, the thesis can be wrapped in a 'story' and passed on (brokered).

This is why we guide TOPS contributors to write up each of their ideas by explaining it in terms of value and catalysts.

But you need to be careful with this approach. In his book *The Signal and the Noise*, Nate Silver explains why and how TV investment pundits make for such bad investors. By the time a story becomes so well packaged that it can be pumped on CNBC or at

Breakers or the Sohn Conference it is probably too late. The interesting moment is when the idea is just in its dawn, half-glimpsed and half-understood.

Storytelling is only interesting in the genesis of an idea, not in its recounting months later. At Marshall Wace we use 'narrative investor' as a pejorative term. For years, the hedge fund industry has been under the spell of the Tiger Cub model, a term used to refer to investors who grew up under the aprons of, or were funded by, Julian Robertson's Tiger Fund. It is true that several great investors emerged from the Tiger pool. But the model brought with it a lot of hubris and misplaced hero worship. Tiger Cubs hunted in packs, ramping their stocks at Breakers and at the Sohn Conference. Investors fawned. Some funds of funds even invented a model to follow the managers into the individual stocks, doubling up on the herding problem.

What everyone should know is that it is very easy to tell a story about a stock. Your ability to tell a story has almost nothing to do with your ability to pick stocks. In the case of some successful managers, it is almost inversely correlated. Yet it is the staple, still, of many due diligence processes. By all means ask questions about stocks for entertainment and to illustrate the process of the manager. But don't give it much weight in your due diligence.

The alternative approach to catalyst-based investing is to take the view that markets are intrinsically bad at discounting long-term growth and earnings streams, and therefore that the optimum strategy is to buy and hold quality companies. These companies also typically have the advantage of lower volatility and therefore, on a risk-adjusted basis, this model might give superior returns over time. Many successful careers have been built on this long-term growth strategy, especially in emerging markets.

However, it is essentially lazy. The implicit assumption is that the Competitive Advantage Period of a company (the period during which a company can enjoy superior returns on investment before they fade) will last longer than the market expects and therefore offers an anomaly to be exploited. Arguably the model was pioneered by Philip Fisher, who was himself a great influence on Buffett (Buffett credited him with 15 per cent of all he had learned about investing; the other 85 per cent went to Ben Graham). Fisher sought out companies which were both 'fortunate' (in their industry structure and market growth) and 'able' (as defined by management strength). This combination would assure super-normal returns on capital over the long term and represented the best core criteria for long-term investments. We leaned heavily on Philip Fisher's ideas when we launched the Eureka Fund and designated about one-third of our capital for such 'core' holdings.

However, this approach is increasingly hard to apply in an Age of Disruption where few business models survive the scrutiny of competition for very long. Warren Buffett made famous the idea of 'moats' protecting a company's pricing power, and the weakness of US monopoly law means that many US moats last longer than they should. But Jeff Bezos now seeks out any companies with moats with the ruthlessness of a surgeon. As he has said, 'Your margin is my opportunity'.

The best that can be said today is that the market is not good at predicting Competitive Advantage Periods and frequently errs in both underestimating and overestimating the speed of change. Scrutiny of industry structure and sector dynamics can generate super-normal returns from industry selection because not enough investors do it.

LESSON 6
THE BEST PORTFOLIO CONSTRUCTION COMBINES CONCENTRATION WITH DIVERSIFICATION

It is a rule applicable to every good fund manager: over time the more concentrated the portfolio, the higher the return. Whatever they may say, very few managers have a high conviction at any one time about more than about ten stocks. They simply don't have the bandwidth to analyse enough stocks to retain more than about ten high conviction names 'on the boil'. So they should concentrate their risk where their conviction lies – in those top names.

That is why Marshall Wace designed the TOPS system so that no contributor was permitted to run more than ten to fifteen names in his/her virtual portfolio at any one time. It is also why we expect our own fundamental managers to run concentrated portfolios (30–50 longs). Focusing on highest conviction ideas brings the best results.

Even with 30–50 long positions, it is not uncommon (and is fully embraced) for just ten names to make up close to 100 per cent of the idiosyncratic risk of a discretionary manager. Managers may carry more positions, but they should be dynamically sizing those positions on a continuous basis to optimise risk concentration.

In the early days of Eureka, we frequently carried single position sizes of up to 20 per cent of fund NAV and risk.

To make concentration really work in a portfolio you need to be sure that as many of your positions as possible are working for you. You cannot afford many 'sleepers'. And you need a high 'slugging ratio'. This is another baseball analogy. While the success ratio from Lesson 3, or 'batting average', is calculated as the ratio of the *number* of winning (or positive alpha) trades to losing trades, the slugging ratio is calculated based on the realised *gains* on winning trades compared to realised losses on losing trades. It is also known as the 'win/loss ratio', and maximising your slugging ratio is a key skill of a successful trader. The best exponent of this is probably Stanley Druckenmiller. Druckenmiller is a believer in concentration and has strong, non-consensual, convictions. But he uses technical indicators (i.e. price charts) to seek confirmation from the market that his ideas are performing, and waits to size up his positions until he gets confirmation from the price action.

While concentration maximises your absolute return, one of the keys to delivering outstanding risk-adjusted returns is diversification.

The law of portfolio diversification is that rare beast – a genuinely helpful innovation to have come out of the Chicago School. Harry Markowitz introduced Modern Portfolio Theory in 1952, in an essay for which he later received the Nobel Prize. The key insight was that an investor could reduce portfolio risk simply by holding combinations of instruments which were not perfectly correlated. Modern portfolio theory is really the foundation stone of the fund management industry and it has been the foundation of many successful fund management businesses. But like all great insights or innovations, it has also been misused when it has fallen into the wrong hands.

At its best, diversification allows you to enhance the risk-adjusted returns of a pool of good assets. The problem is that diversification also looks like it works to improve the risk characteristics of bad assets, in short runs of data. Over the longer term, we tend to discover that bad assets are more correlated than one might have expected, because they share a common factor – they are all bad! Thus, in the 1980s, Michael Milken used diversification as the foundational rationale for the junk bond market. And then, even more calamitously, diversification was what

LESSON 6

allowed banks in the 2000s to combine securitised junk mortgages into CDOs and CDO-squared and to sell them on as higher-quality credits. Innovation can always be used for good or ill. The tool of diversification is so powerful that it has unfortunately been used too often for ill.

As anyone can spot, the merits of concentration and diversification stand in paradox and almost in contradiction. A more concentrated portfolio brings higher return while diversification brings lower risk but also dilutes return.

Famously Warren Buffett disagreed with Ben Graham about the value of diversification. Graham was a staunch advocate of diversification. Buffett dismissed it: 'Diversification is protection against ignorance. It makes little sense if you know what you are doing.'

How can these two perspectives be reconciled?

The answer is that you cannot fully reconcile them at the level of a single portfolio – there are trade-offs between concentration and diversification, between return and risk. But you can reconcile them at the level of the business and at the level of the client.

The blending of concentration and diversification lies at the heart of the Marshall Wace business model.

In the case of TOPS, the individual contributor portfolios are typically limited to ten ideas – maximising concentration. But when those ideas are combined at the level of the client portfolio, we create portfolios with thousands of positions. Thus clients benefit from maximum diversification. But they also receive all the benefits of concentration – namely the maximum conviction of every underlying contributor. We combine maximum conviction with maximum diversification.

The same trick can be performed in a multi-manager fund and no doubt explains why multi-manager funds or 'platform funds' are becoming one of the most successful corners of the hedge fund industry. In the case of our flagship fund, Eureka, each underlying sub-portfolio is concentrated.

LESSON 6

The correlation between the different sub-portfolios is less than 0.2×. By being able to combine such low correlation return streams we create a highly diversified fund and ensure substantial uplift to the Sharpe Ratio. The fund maximises its return per unit of risk.

LESSON 7
SHORTS ARE DIFFERENT FROM LONGS

So might have said Forrest Gump. But it needs stating even if it is obvious.

Most managers find alpha easier to come by from their long positions than their shorts. By way of a proxy for the industry, in the ten years to December 2018, the Eureka Fund (which comprises roughly fifteen strategies in all global regions and sectors) annualised gross long alpha of 8.79 per cent and gross short alpha of 2.81 per cent.

There are many reasons why alpha is easier to generate on the long side. The first is that the informational bias of the market is entirely structured against the short seller. Companies publish information which will cast them in the best light and hide the bad news. Brokers have an incentive to please quoted companies in order to gain access to management or even to gain business for their investment banking arm. This is reflected in the balance of published broker reports, which are overwhelmingly (70:30 or 80:20) skewed to Buy/Hold over Sell recommendations.

Reflecting these manifold biases, the best short sellers rightly see themselves as crusaders for truth or as Robin Hood figures pitted against the stock market establishment.

But there are also a host of technical reasons why shorting is more difficult:

1. **Short positions are much more expensive to hold than long positions**. When you short a stock you have to post collateral, pay the cost of borrow and fabricate any dividends foregone. Over the ten years to December 2018, the normalised cost of loan fees for the Eureka Fund was 48 basis points. This represents a significant 'negative

carry'. In contrast, long positions have a positive carry (the dividend plus any buyback) which rewards a fairly passive buy and hold approach. The alpha from short positions has to be considered net of borrowing costs to make it comparable in financial terms to the alpha on longs.

2. **Shorting is more competitive.** Essentially on the short side you are competing with hedge funds, the self-selected elite of the fund management industry. When you short sell a stock, you may be pitting your wits against the whole market – the buyer could be an active long fund, a passive fund or a hedge fund – but in the borrowing market you are up only against hedge funds. That means the price and availability of borrow will be determined by a highly competitive market. Crowdedness of short positions is a positive signal for alpha (i.e. crowded shorts go down by more than the market) but the popularity of the short will usually be reflected in the cost of borrow.

3. **Short alpha is regime dependent**. It is stronger in bear markets than bull markets. There are fundamental reasons for this. In a bull market, poor companies and weak balance sheets are often bailed out by central bank profligacy, asset price inflation or investor animal spirits. They find it possible (sometimes easy) to raise capital to restore the balance sheet. Shale oil companies, for example, were able to ride a wave of over-confidence in the US for years with negative cash flow and over-leveraged balance sheets in the knowledge that they could – and did – raise new equity almost overnight at only a small discount to the prevailing share price. In a bear market, the ability to raise equity disappears (except at hugely dilutive prices) and weak balance sheets are suddenly penalised. In a bull market, weak companies are often bailed out by corporate activity. In a bear market, M&A activity drains away.

And the problem for the short seller is that bull markets last longer than bear markets. In the past 50 years there have been six bull markets and six bear markets, if you define a bear market as a 20 per cent drawdown which is not reversed for twelve months. The average bull market has lasted 6.9 years, the average bear market 1.5 years. Being a dedicated short seller is a vocation – it is certainly not a great career choice.

4. **Short selling is more risky**. Unlike long positions, where you can lose at most the amount invested in the equity, the potential loss on a short position is theoretically unlimited. Short sellers also risk margin calls, regulatory changes (such as a short sale ban) and potential increases in loan fees.

5. **Short positions need to be traded more actively than longs**. This is especially true as weak companies approach the distressed end of their lives. Operational distress in a company will often lead to financial stress and to higher financial leverage. As a stock becomes more financially leveraged its financial performance and outlook become more uncertain and the share price more volatile. This may be compounded by the

crowdedness of the short position and the skittishness of other investors. Effectively the Sharpe Ratio of the trade is likely to fall.

It is highly tempting to short a stock as it approaches its death throes. As one market aphorism goes, the definition of a stock which falls 90 per cent is a stock which falls 80 per cent and then halves. However, shorting a company in its death throes can be a highly treacherous exercise. Even if it gives intellectual satisfaction to track the shares to zero, the sweet spot for shorting is often much earlier, when the full weakness of the company has yet to fully emerge and the Sharpe Ratio of the short position is much higher.

6. **When a short position goes against you it grows in size and becomes more of a problem for your portfolio**. On the other hand, when a long goes against you it becomes smaller and therefore less of a problem. The natural discipline on the long side if a position goes against you and your conviction is unchanged is to add to the

position, thereby 'averaging down'. This does not work on the short side. If a position goes against you it grows and becomes a bigger position automatically. You cannot 'average up' without the position becoming super-sized.

To be a truly successful short seller you need to actively pursue the criteria which are specific to a great short. The first three examples below are just the reverse image of successful longs. The final two are unique to the short side:

1. **Weak or deteriorating growth** (e.g. due to demographic factors, fashion, disruption, technology change).

2. **Industry structure** (i.e. a weak or deteriorating industry structure). The trend of many industries is towards concentration and improved pricing power. This is because most management teams are keen to implement the lessons they have imbibed at business school from Michael Porter,

Warren Buffett and others and to create moats around their business and consolidate their markets. Industry consolidation leads to stronger pricing power.

However, we also live in an era of almost unparalleled creative destruction, driven especially but not only by the forces of digital disruption, and this has created countervailing forces which have plunged many industries into a spiral of falling prices and falling demand.

The scale of disruption across so many industries (from retail to advertising to autos) has made this type of creative destruction a rich source of short ideas. Timing can often be challenging. As Bill Gates said, we always overestimate the change that will occur in the next two years and underestimate the change that will occur in the next ten. However, patience invariably rewards long-term structural shorts premised on inexorable changes in industry structure.

3. **Regulatory pressure** (a hostile regulatory or political framework which is likely

to further pressurise earnings power). Most US companies spend a lot of money making sure the regulatory environment is supportive. The annual lobbying bill in Washington DC is circa $2 billion. But when political fashion is strong enough, some industries simply can't escape the wrath of the regulator. Tobacco and Big Pharma are most in the firing line at the moment.

4. **Dodgy accounting**. Market scrutiny is such that few companies attempt to play games with their accounting. But cases still exist, more frequently in emerging than developed markets. Such cases require great patience as shorts because the payback may be non-existent for years and then very sudden. The caprice of time is reminiscent of Mike Campbell, Hemingway's anti-hero in *The Sun Also Rises*. Campbell was a former bankrupt. When asked how he went bankrupt, he replied: 'Two ways. Gradually, then suddenly.'

5. **Weak and deteriorating balance sheets**. Weak balance sheets can be a dangerous

temptation on the short side, especially in an era of unlimited monetary support. Central banks can keep zombie companies alive for many years, preventing the forces of creative destruction from properly operating.

But weak balance sheets can also deliver the best shorts. Financial leverage massively increases the potential downside in a share.

The natural conclusion is that the weak balance sheet is not enough. It has to be weak *and* deteriorating. If a company is operationally and financially challenged, the downside can be considerable, even starting from a low point.

LESSON 8
A MACHINE BEATS A MAN, BUT A MAN PLUS A MACHINE BEATS A MACHINE

Like any good aphorism, this one has many parents. It is most often attributed to Gary Kasparov after his narrow defeat by Big Blue, although what he actually said was:

'Human strategic guidance combined with the tactical acuity of a computer is overwhelming.'

In 2016, DeepMind's AlphaGo became the first computer programme to defeat a professional human Go player. The Chinese game Go was seen as much more complex than chess, and DeepMind's victory as a level up. But investing in complex non-linear markets with millions of daily transactions is a different level altogether from either chess or Go. So if the aphorism applies anywhere it applies to financial markets.

Marshall Wace's equity business is divided almost evenly between systematic (quant) and fundamental (discretionary) investing. So we are in an almost unique position to judge the merits of machines, of the two approaches to investment and of their potential for combination.

Systematic investing has made huge advances in recent years, to the point where some are predicting the imminent eclipse of traditional fundamental investing.

It has been possible with machines to identify a range of factors (or 'risk premia') hitherto bundled up in the discretionary process which can be replicated by computers. Perhaps ironically, many of the techniques used to identify these factors were based on the work of the theorist of efficient markets himself, Eugene Fama. AQR were the pioneers of this approach and have deservedly built a great business upon the use of style factors to generate systematic returns. Some style factors, such as momentum and value, have delivered consistently positive alpha. As these factors can be easily replicated, machines have been able to invade the space, eroding the definition of what can be attributed to human skill.

For most hedge fund allocators, the skill which they are prepared to reward with proper performance fees is confined to 'idiosyncratic alpha' (i.e. that which cannot be explained or replicated by these factors).

The definition of non-idiosyncratic (or 'common') factors is expanding rapidly though, as machines increase their penetration of the markets, and can now include factors like long crowding, short crowding, long-only crowding, even market sentiment. As we discussed in Lesson 3, some allocators and managers even include sector selection as a common factor, although there is no evidence yet that it is being replicated successfully by machines.

The march of the machines is also encroaching on even more proprietary aspects of fundamental investing. It is now possible to use machines to systematically analyse the reported accounts of every listed company in order to identify improving and deteriorating patterns.

All kinds of other data sources can be mined for systematic alpha signals, including broker sentiment, market sentiment, social media sentiment, fund flows and market positioning. All this has been happening for years and machines are much better equipped to process these vast amounts of data and generate alpha signals from them than any human.

In this sense, systematic investing is most certainly encroaching on the space hitherto occupied by discretionary investing and using data in a precise and effective way that fundamental investors had hitherto only been capturing intuitively and without precision.

The machines will continue to improve – in coverage and in processing power. Machine learning and AI now drive a significant part of our systematic process and their share will continue to grow, expanding the range of signals we can use and accelerating the speed at which we translate the data into signals and the signals into trades.

But machines have not won yet. Machines typically do not fare well in a crisis. They are not good at responding to a new paradigm until the rules of the new paradigm are plugged into them by a human. During the Brexit referendum or around the Trump presidential election our discretionary traders fared much better than our systematic business as they were better suited to make the leap of imagination to understand the implications of what had just happened.

Discretionary managers are also much better equipped to vary their risk budgets, to recognise a slam dunk and to make the leap in risk appetite which allows them to make a lot of money once every few years.

Systematic investing typically operates on the basis of diversification and multiplication (many positions, many trades) whereas fundamental investors rely on concentration and amplification (a small number of concentrated positions with lower turnover).

Maybe machines will find a way to close this gap in portfolio construction, but they will always lag in understanding new paradigms and therefore always lag behind on the really big trades.

At the time of writing, systematic hedge funds are in the midst of a protracted period of poor performance (15 months plus). The world of systematic investing is becoming more competitive and yet alpha opportunities do not yet seem to have eroded much on the fundamental side. Perhaps there is room for both.

What is also certainly true is that the two will increasingly converge. Our fundamental managers are making ever greater use of the immense data resources of our systematic side and using them to facilitate and improve decision making. There is no reason why technology cannot be a huge boon to the productivity of fundamental investing.

There is also a space between fundamental and systematic investing which we have chosen to call Quantamental. Quantamental is about the sourcing of new 'alternative data sets' which can be used to provide additional insights to discretionary managers and to provide extra conviction to the mosaic they are building around a stock.

The extra alpha insights, whether they be around credit data, sales, traffic, output, sentiment, brand strength or social media sentiment, all add to the picture a manager is able to build about a stock and help him/her to take a sizeable position.

Quantamental sits between fundamental and systematic because it uses Big Data from new sources and enables our fundamental managers to combine this with a set of other insights to build high conviction positions, which translate into concentrated portfolios.

The three approaches to investing – Fundamental, Systematic and Quantamental – may well converge further. What all three are going to have in common is a huge and growing reliance on technology and Big Data. An important part of the competitive race will be data acquisition and processing power. Akin to Moore's Law, or the speed of improvement in processing power which is driving the genomics revolution, technology will play a determining part in competitive advantage for investing. Those firms willing to invest will have a good chance of winning. Those unwilling to invest will fall by the wayside.

Marshall Wace processes 150 petabytes of data each month, which equates to 7.5 petabytes per day. In reality, and depending on the definition of data processing, this number could be much higher were it to include all of the operations performed within the processes themselves. And this number is almost doubling every year. In three years' time we expect to be processing over 20 petabytes per day. The ability to harness and deploy technology and data will be one of the most important determinants of long-term competitiveness in the investment industry.

LESSON 9
RISK MANAGEMENT – RESPECT UNCERTAINTY

'There are old soldiers and there are bold soldiers but there are no old, bold soldiers', as the highly decorated US Army colonel David Hackworth wrote in his memoir, *About Face*.

According to Hackworth, the keys to being a good soldier sound similar to those to being a good investor:

> [I]nsight, receptivity and risk management. It takes insight to formulate a battle plan or thesis, receptivity to change the battle plan as the facts and circumstances change and risk management to avoid large losses and/or commit your resources to the most vital parts of

the battle – proper risk management is how you become an old soldier.

(David Hackworth, *About Face*, 1989)

There are many parallels between military strategy and investing. Both involve complex systems dependent on human agency – multiple decisions with multiple outcomes including a significant element of chance. But also reflexivity – one set of actions by one participant can change the reality of the market/battle and therefore change the behaviour of other participants.

Principles of engagement and heuristics only go so far in battle, as they do in markets. As German Field Marshal Von Moltke put it: 'In war as in art there exist no general rules; in neither can talent be replaced by precept.' The second ingredient cited by Hackworth, receptivity, is vital, because in markets (as in battle) you constantly have to react to emergent phenomena, to new developments.

But the parallels between markets and the battlefield only go so far. The battlefield is much easier, even if the stakes are higher.

LESSON 9

In battle there are usually just two protagonists (the opposing generals), each trying to impose order on complexity. If you can understand and anticipate the protagonists, you will go a long way to anticipating the outcomes.

In markets there are multiple protagonists at multiple levels, all of whom can impact outcomes. Yes, there are governments and central banks who might try to impose centralised order in times of extreme crisis, but barring these interventions, you are operating within a near-perfect example of multi-agent non-linear complexity.

This poses the challenge of what can be predicted – and prepared for – and what cannot.

On the question of the nature of predictability, there has been a longstanding debate in the field of mathematics and probability which mirrors the arguments around Enlightenment economics we discussed back in Lesson 1.

On the one hand are traditional Bayesians, for whom all probabilities should be quantifiable even in conditions of uncertainty. At the other end of the spectrum are thinkers like Keynes and Frank Knight who argued for a concept which has come to be known as Radical Uncertainty.

In his 1921 *Treatise on Probability*, Keynes claimed that there were some things which were simply unknowable and which therefore could not be ascribed probabilities:

> By uncertain knowledge, I do not mean merely to distinguish what is known for certain from what is only probable. The sense in which I am using the term is that in which the prospect of a European war is uncertain... There is no scientific basis to form any calculable probability whatever. We simply do not know.

Ten years later, Knight drew a distinction between known risks which could be probabilised and unmeasurable uncertainties which simply could not be contained within a Bayesian calculus:

LESSON 9

Uncertainty must be taken in a sense radically distinct from the familiar notion of Risk, from which it has never been properly separated.... The essential fact is that 'risk' means in some cases a quantity susceptible of measurement, while at other times it is something distinctly not of this character; and there are far-reaching and crucial differences in the bearings of the phenomena depending on which of the two is really present and operating.... It will appear that a measurable uncertainty, or 'risk' proper, as we shall use the term, is so far different from an unmeasurable one that it is not in effect an uncertainty at all.

(Frank Knight, *Risk, Uncertainty and Profit*, 1921)

Fundamental to Keynes and Knight was the understanding that many things are simply not knowable. Donald Rumsfeld has popularised the concept more recently in a military context with his idea of 'known unknowns' and 'unknown unknowns'. This concept also underpins Nassim Taleb's idea of 'Black Swans', the singular events which falsify a theory no matter how many past observations might have supported it.

More recently, Mervyn King made radical uncertainty a key theme in his analysis of the 2008 crisis.

> In a world of radical uncertainty there is no way of identifying the probabilities of future events and no set of equations that describes people's attempt to cope with, rather than optimize against, that uncertainty. ... In the latter world, the economic relationships between money, income, saving and interest rates are unpredictable, although they are the outcome of attempts by rational people to cope with an uncertain world.

The application of this uncertainty principle to risk management is, in a way, not so complicated. On one level, known risks need to be constantly quantified, probability-weighted and modelled, and portfolios stressed against those scenarios, using historic simulation where possible.

On the other level, newly 'emergent phenomena' (previously-unknown unknowns) need to be anticipated, identified, contextualised, modelled, turned into new stress scenarios.

The art of risk management is to anticipate or identify emergent risks so you are ahead of the wave before it breaks. The science is to probability-weight those risks and stress-test portfolios in real time so you can anticipate the effect of the wave on your portfolio.

It also matters how you stress the portfolios. Traditional parametric VaR (value at risk) stress tests assume that returns and volatility follow a normal distribution. They are useful in normalised environments. But in stressed environments? Not so much. They need to be supplemented with empirical stress tests which use historical data as far as it goes back. This enables you to capture – at least partially – the extreme moves which occur in tail events, which happen far more frequently than models imply. Each tail event is different and history never repeats itself exactly, but at least it enables a better understanding of the scale of movement and the varying nature of relationships between securities.

The challenge of combining art and science is at its most acute in times of crisis. Richard Bookstaber, formerly responsible for risk management at Morgan Stanley and Bridgewater, among others, describes the heart of risk management in a period of crisis as follows:

> When I've been in the middle of a crisis like the 1987 crash, I am sitting around a table with the various characters working through a story line; as a crisis evolves we are trying to fit a narrative to the events and develop a good, supportable plot line going forward. The effective model is a tool for developing these qualitative narratives, not a machine that spits out numbers onto the table. ...The decision makers pose a narrative and then test it

for believability – is the plot line a reasonable one?

(Richard Bookstaber, *The End of Theory*, 2017)

Bookstaber's use of the word 'narrative' is not accidental. In a crisis, two things are going on. There are the events (the drivers of the crisis) and there are the market actors' responses, which themselves reflexively influence the unfolding of events. The actors' responses are driven not only by fundamentals but also by competing narratives. Fundamentals can shift on a daily basis as policy makers intervene or market practitioners act (reflexively or otherwise) and so the precious skill is to anticipate the narrative which approximates what is going on and which is going to drive investor behaviour.

In a world of radical uncertainty, pragmatism and flexibility become the essential skills. You can harness the rules-based systems and Bayesian models, but the art needs ultimately to be in charge of the science.

To return to military parallels, one of the most interesting military strategists of recent decades is Colonel John Boyd, a much-decorated US pilot who served in the Korean war and after in the Pentagon. Radical uncertainty was his stock in trade. At a 1992 address to the Air War College he warned of the dangers of rigidity: 'The Air Force has got a doctrine, the Army's got a doctrine, Navy's got a doctrine, everybody's got a doctrine.' But of his own work he said, 'doctrine doesn't appear in there even once. You can't find it. You know why I don't have it in there? Because it's doctrine on day one, and every day after it becomes dogma.' ... 'if you got one doctrine, you're a dinosaur. Period.'

Richard Bookstaber's conclusion is that the way to deal with a constantly changing world, ever in flux, is through agent-based modelling.

Agent-based modelling allows for the complexity of the real world – for multiple agents, emergent phenomena, randomness, actions and reactions. In its purest form this does not mean abstract modelling which reduces the agents to arbitrary categories but rather it means understanding the specifics of each major financial agent – central banks, governments, Blackrock, Goldman, Bridgewater, Citadel, AQR, AIG, etc. – and the way they may act or react in specific circumstances.

Embracing the idea of radical uncertainty has significant consequences for the way you structure investment portfolios and specifically for the way you manage liquidity and leverage.

Hedge funds have to be structured in the good times to make the maximum return per unit of risk but also to take account of the dangers of unknown unknowns occurring at any time.

Known unknowns can typically be hedged through cheap 'tail protection'. An Italian financial meltdown could be hedged through CDS protection on Italian banks or sovereign bonds. A Chinese financial implosion could be hedged through options or forward trades in the Renminbi. A collapse of confidence in the efficacy of central bank policy could be hedged through options or futures in gold.

But these are conventional known unknowns. The radical uncertainty principle also requires us to think about the unknown unknowns which we have simply not thought to hedge.

The best hedge against unknown unknowns is structural prudence in the use of liquidity and leverage.

Liquidity and leverage are the two grim reapers of the financial markets. They drive the forced selling which turns a crisis into a rout, whether that be through liquidity mismatches, margin calls or leverage withdrawals. And they bring down the curtain on poor investment managers.

This means that you have to set ceilings on both ('prudential margins') which allow for those unexpected tail events.

Leverage
Leverage is a very good tool when applied in moderation. The Capital Asset Pricing

Model (a perfectly good piece of Enlightenment economics) teaches us that there is a healthy balance to be struck between debt and equity capital and that a managed use of debt enhances returns.

The problem arises when investors become so enamoured with the investment proposition that they layer on excessive levels of debt.

In the investment world, many of the worst financial accidents of the last 30 years can be traced back to this type of financial hubris.

The stories of junk bonds and CDOs have much in common. As we briefly discussed in Lesson 6, both took a very powerful innovation (Markowitz's model of diversification) and used it to transform a financial market. But in both cases, investors got carried away with the investment proposition and took it too far.

Michael Milken was the pioneer of junk bonds. By wrapping lots of highly leveraged debt instruments together in a diversified bundle, the law of diversification meant he de-risked the junk. So investors piled in. And some added extra leverage. But diversified junk is still junk and so when the US hit a corporate recession, the leverage became a bane rather than a boon. It didn't help that crime was also involved.

The 2008 crisis was almost a repetition of the junk bond fiasco. The law of diversification was applied to turn junk mortgages into triple A CDOs. And banks were so pleased with the outcomes that they created CDOs-squared. Leverage upon leverage. A good idea (diversification) carried far beyond the bounds of common sense and prudence.

Many investing institutions, and especially hedge funds, use the same Markowitz rules of diversification to very profitable effect. Diversification maximises return per unit of risk. One big difference between hedge funds and junk bonds or CDOs is that hedge funds are not leveraging junk (at least not intentionally). They are leveraging quality diversified investments.

Most of our investment funds are built on a model of diversified low-correlated alpha streams. In the case of our flagship fund, Eureka, this is explicitly the case. All the component streams are intended to have high Sharpe Ratios in their own right.

The level of diversification enables us to apply extra leverage to the funds while still generating only very modest volatility. The maximum leverage of any Marshall Wace fund (defined as gross longs plus gross short/NAV) is 400 per cent.

Some clients push us to take more leverage, to match some of our peers, such as Citadel and Millennium, who run gross leverage typically around 600–700 per cent. These funds would argue that they can afford to take more leverage because they run such strict parameters at the level of their sub-strategies in terms of market neutrality and the elimination of non-idiosyncratic risk.

This makes us uneasy. One definition of idiosyncratic risk as discussed above is 'anything that cannot be explained or replicated by models'. But the frontier of what is explicable is moving all the time. So we don't trust idiosyncratic risk. There are risk factors which we don't understand or model today which we may understand tomorrow. There are unknown unknowns, which may surprise our risk models.

Equity markets are now frequently punctuated by de-leveraging episodes, as levered hedge funds hit their drawdown limits (which are essential disciplines) and cut their books. This is happening at a time of central bank profligacy when markets are still trending up. What would happen in a crisis? Or when central banks are less supportive?

In relation to leverage, you always need to leave yourself enough prudential margin to survive a crisis. The definition of prudential margin is a situation where you are able to take advantage of other players' distress rather than leaving them to take advantage of yours.

Liquidity

The most notorious liquidity-induced crisis was the 1987 crash, caused by portfolio insurance. Because market participants

LESSON 9

were not excessively leveraged, the market bounced back quickly and the crash did not have long-term consequences.

Liquidity problems are more often specific to individual funds or fund managers rather than the market as a whole, and particularly when a fund becomes oversized in individual positions and unable to exit without a forced sale.

Most commonly, liquidity problems at the stock level can be compounded by excessive leverage at the fund level or by mismatches between position liquidity and fund liquidity.

In 2008, many hedge funds got into difficulty because of the mismatch between the liquidity terms of their funds and the liquidity of their underlying positions. Their investors wanted out and they could not raise the necessary liquidity. As a result, many funds 'gated' their investors, effectively blocking redemptions. In some cases, this may have been in the clients' long-term interest (in terms of value recovery) but in most cases it was not. Even in the best cases it is an indictment of the manager that they did not hold the prudential level of liquidity to deal with unknown unknowns.

Clients should never be asked to pay such a price. In some cases, clients literally had to pay the price, continuing to pay the management fee while the fund was gated. This may have been legal but it was a disgrace to the fund management industry.

There is no mathematical rule for the right level of 'prudential liquidity'. Ian likes to say, 'never be in a position where the stock owns you'. In other words, never be in a position where you lose your flexibility to exit. And that includes making allowances for a crisis environment.

With $120 billion of gross balance sheet in global equities, we could be in danger of pushing at some of these limits. So we operate with tight rules. As a firm, we never own more than 5 per cent of the free float of any one company, no matter how much we like the investment. We also impose tight limits on the share of any portfolio in stocks with lower liquidity profiles.

LESSON 10
SIZE MATTERS

Any investment business needs a certain critical mass of assets under management (AuM), not only to pay for the light bulbs but also to pay for a minimum level of research and execution capability. The entry barriers are rising and it has been estimated that the minimum scale of AuM required for a hedge fund to break even has risen sevenfold, from $50m in 1998 to $350m in 2018.

But the guilty secret of the fund management business is that size matters even more in the other direction. Beyond a certain level of AuM, size becomes an impediment to skill-based returns as it raises trading costs in a non-linear fashion and reduces the flexibility of trading and risk management.

One of the most formative experiences of

my investment career was to watch from the sidelines as my UK colleagues at Mercury Asset Management grew their equities business to be the largest and most successful in the UK, but then grew to be simply too big, owning huge (10 per cent plus) holdings in many of the leading FTSE stocks and so becoming unable to vary their exposures easily without the whole market being aware. The team included many exceptionally talented fund managers. But they were too big for the market. Eventually (in 1998) the firm's UK performance blew up completely.

The pattern has repeated itself many times, most recently in the case of Woodford Investment management in the UK. It is a pattern familiar from any number of hedge funds:

Julian Robertson was the almost legendary manager of the Tiger Fund. He annualised circa 25 per cent per annum during the 20-year life of his fund from 1980 and became a billionaire. But this would not have been your investor experience, especially if you were late to the party. The money-weighted return on the fund since inception was relatively modest. Robertson allowed the fund to grow to $13 billion but did not adapt the way he ran money, which was through a concentrated high conviction portfolio. In its last three years the fund lost 4 per cent (1998), 19 per cent (1999) and 13 per cent before it was decided to close it down in 2000. Some of the positions were so large and unwieldy that Robertson decided to distribute them *in specie* to clients rather than unwind in the market, most famously his 22.4 per cent stake in US Airways.

There are natural limits to the size of any investment strategy. We measure them in two main ways:

1. **Execution costs.** These can be measured and predicted. At a certain level of AuM, trading costs begin to scale in a non-linear fashion and this represents a meaningful handicap to realised returns. The only exception to this is strategies where the turnover is sufficiently low that the hurdle is only ever modest. But low turnover (defined, say, as less

than 3× per year) strategies generally do not generate the kind of supra-normal alpha that we need to deliver on our client expectations.

From our experience, execution costs typically lead to a fundamental equity strategy being capped anywhere from $1–3 billion in capital. Most good managers can deliver strong alpha on up to $1 billion of capital. Very few can deliver the same persistently above $3 billion.

For systematic strategies it is possible to scale much higher. The extent of diversification (1000+ names per portfolio) means that each position represents a much smaller share of daily trading.

2. **Liquidity footprint.** Even if a fund is traded relatively slowly, the size of AuM can lead a manager to own an excessive share of a company's free float. This may not matter for months or even years, but in times of crisis, the manager can find him/herself unable to trade out of the position without a significant discount. This is amplified when the excessive footprint applies across many

LESSON 10

stocks and even more so when the market knows about it and can punish the manager.

This liquidity risk can only be avoided by applying a prudential approach to the amount of any company free float which the fund/firm can own (see Lesson 8). And this in turn leads to upper bounds on individual fund size – if a manager's natural hunting ground is in the mid-cap arena and they naturally own large stakes in individual companies, the fund should be automatically capped at the point where there is still a prudential liquidity margin for the uncertainty of a financial crisis.

We define liquidity primarily as a percentage of a stock's trading volume rather than a percentage of market cap or free float, as it is the former which matters more in most circumstances. However, we monitor and restrict both. Given that all our strategies are subject to drawdown limits, all have to work on the basis that they could at any stage become a forced seller – even the best long-term committed position may one day become part of an investment liquidation.

LESSON 10½
MOST FUND MANAGEMENT CAREERS END IN FAILURE

All political lives, unless they are cut off in midstream at a happy juncture, end in failure, because that is the nature of politics and of human affairs.

What Enoch Powell said about politics is even more true of fund management.

Politics has an almost inevitable cycle of popularity to it, insofar as the people can fall in and out of love with even their most popular tribunes – as Churchill discovered in 1945.

Fund managers are not as immediately exposed to the same democratic process. They don't stand for election. But they are indirectly exposed to the whims of popularity in ways which magnify its effects. When a fund manager is popular, investors rush to their fund, pumping it up to a size which makes it increasingly challenging to deliver the same return per unit of risk. When a fund manager loses his or her halo, investors can vote with their feet (unless they are gated), pushing the fund manager into forced liquidation and unleashing a negative spiral of poor performance and subsequent liquidation.

But these are technical arguments. There are deeper reasons why most fund management careers end in failure and they relate mainly to character.

We have already established that even a really good fund manager is wrong with at least 45 per cent of his or her trades and is bound to have periods – sometimes quite extended – of poor performance. It matters enormously how the fund manager reacts to these poor periods. The combination of client pressure and peer pressure can be intense. You need deep reserves of resilience. Confidence in your convictions. Confidence in yourself to come through the valley. A strong character will use the period of underperformance to lay the foundation for the next period of good performance, by re-examining every assumption, every thesis, discarding some and doubling down on others. A weak character will freeze, their decision-making impaired. Or they might take flight, mentally at least, and avoid the difficult thinking.

Fund managers often exit the business on one of these points of failure, either because they are forced out stupidly by clients or employers (like Tony Dye in 1999 at the peak of the internet bubble) or because they lose heart or energy.

Other fund managers fail for the equal and opposite character flaw – hubris. They extrapolate their own strong performance, build false confidence, begin to discard advice. The structure of the hedge fund industry lends itself to this. Hedge funds have a star structure. Entry barriers are, or used to be, low, requiring limited capital. Many firms ended up being fully owned and controlled by a single individual. It is very easy, if you are the single owner of the business, to become impatient of advice, blind to your own limitations, weary of democratic decision-making. Additionally, you may have become rich and flattered and confuse your wealth with your worth (more of a danger in the US, where wealth is admired, than the UK, where wealth is a basis for suspicion).

So you brook increasingly less contradiction and start to make basic mistakes. You allow your fund to grow to a size where it is much more difficult to deliver performance. You allow your positions to grow to a size where they own you rather than you own them.

These two failings of character are a danger in almost any walk of life, but fund management is certainly one of the most prone to them. You need to keep your feet on the ground at all times and always remember that you are never as good or as bad as you (or others) think you are.

The Ancient Romans had a good approach to this. When a general would return home they were typically granted a 'triumph' – it was technically illegal for an army or a general with imperium to enter the city other than at this event – which was effectively a big parade in which the general displayed all of the plunder and captives from the campaign (e.g. elephants from Africa, treasures from Mesopotamia and slaves from Gaul/Britannia/Hispania/Syria/Dacia/Carthage). At the end of the parade, the general would ride in a chariot to be lauded by the crowds lining the streets and to offer a sacrifice at the Temple of Jupiter on Capitoline Hill in the centre of Rome. The general would be accompanied in the chariot by an 'auriga' (a slave with gladiator status). The auriga would continuously whisper in the general's ear *'memento mori'* – 'remember you are mortal'. At the peak of his triumph, the general was reminded of his mortality.

At Marshall Wace, we don't have any aurigae, but we have developed a number of protections against the failings of character. The most important is the partnership structure. Distributed leadership spreads a culture of excellence and of challenge. It also makes each of us dispensable.

Granular performance data makes sure that everyone stays anchored in the reality of their fallibility. The numbers can be cruel but they do not lie. As each of us is wrong on at least 45 per cent of our trades, the data, used correctly, is a guarantor of humility.

Ultimately, of course, it is all about character. If you do not begin your fund management career with a sense of your fallibility, you are likely to learn it. If you do not learn it, you are likely to fail.

GLOSSARY

AuM	assets under management
CDO	collaterised debt obligation
CDS	credit default swap
CRIC	Crisis-Response-Improvement-Complacency
ECB	European Central Bank
EMH	efficient-market hypothesis
LIBOR	London Interbank Offered Rate
LTROs	long-term refinancing operations (of the ECB)
NAV	net asset value
OMTs	outright monetary transactions (of the ECB)
QE	quantitative easing
TLTROs	targeted longer-term refinancing operations (of the ECB)